DON'T TALK JUST KISS
POP MUSIC WISDOM

EDITED AND DESIGNED BY
MARCUS KRAFT

BIS PUBLISHERS

THE GREAT TOPIC OF LOVE HAS PROBABLY BEEN THE MOST
IMPORTANT INSPIRATION FOR SONG WRITERS OF ALL TIMES.
WHEN THINGS GET PARTICULARLY DIFFICULT, AND YOU ARE
LIKELY TO SLIP INTO DESPAIR, SOME OF THE GREATEST POP
SONGS CAN PROVIDE TRUE COMFORT AND HELP YOU TO MAKE
IT THROUGH THE PAIN.

IT ALL BEGAN WHILE I WAS TRAVELLING IN ASIA: IT HAD BEEN
RAINING CATS AND DOGS FOR A WEEK. TO KEEP MY SPIRITS UP,
I LISTENED TO MUSIC, A LOT OF MUSIC. THIS MADE ME REALISE
THAT MANY SONGS GIVE GOOD ADVICE OR PROVIDE WORLDLY
WISDOM. FROM THEN ON, I ASKED EVERY BACKPACKER ON MY TRIP
AND EVERY FRIEND BACK HOME WETHER THEY KNEW SUCH SONGS.
SOON, THE COLLECTION HAD REACHED A REMARKABLE NUMBER...
OVER 500 SONGS. BACK HOME, I ‹HAND PAINTED› EVERY SINGLE
SONG TITLE WITH INK. THE RESULT WAS THE BOOK ‹DON'T
EAT THE YELLOW SNOW›, PUBLISHED IN 2012.

THIS PUBLICATION HERE IS A CONTINUATION: WHILE THE FIRST
BOOK WAS ABOUT WISDOMS IN GENERAL, THIS BOOK EXCLUSIVELY
DEALS WITH ADVICE ON THE SUBJECT OF ‹LOVE›, INCLUDING
EVERYTHING IT ENTAILS: PASSION, TEARS, JOY, DISAPPOINT-
MENT, KISSING, DESIRE, ETC.

YOU'LL FIND 250 OF THE BEST LOVE SONGS FOR TIMES IN
WHICH SOLID ADVICE IS NEEDED. IT'S A COLLECTION OF FAMOUS
SONGS OFFERING ADVICE, BUT IT ALSO CONTAINS MANY
SURPRISES. PLEASE CHECK OUT THE ACCOMPANYING WEBSITE
WWW.POPMUSICWISDOM.COM FOR MORE SONGS.

MARCUS KRAFT
ZURICH, 2017

A GOOD MAN IS HARD TO FIND
ONLY STRANGERS SLEEP IN MY BED
MY FAVORITE WORDS ARE GOODBYE
AND MY FAVORITE COLOR IS RED
— TOM WAITS

A GOOD MAN IS HARD TO FIND

A KISS IS A TERRIBLE THING TO WASTE
YOU SHOULDN'T TREMBLE WHEN WE TOUCH
THERE'S NO REASON FOR THESE FEARS
— MEAT LOAF

A KISS IS A TERRIBLE THING TO WASTE

A KISS IS NOT A CONTRACT
BUT IT'S VERY NICE
JUST BECAUSE YOU'VE BEEN EXPLORING MY MOUTH
DOESN'T MEAN YOU GET
TO TAKE AN EXPEDITION FURTHER SOUTH, NO
— FLIGHT OF THE CONCHORDS

A KISS IS NOT A CONTRACT

A WOMAN CAN CHANGE A MAN
IF SHE LOVES HIM, THE WAY THAT I'M IN LOVE WITH YOU
I KNOW IT, I KNOW THAT I CAN
IF IT'S THE LAST THING, THE LAST THING I'D EVER DO
— BONEY M

A WOMAN CAN CHANGE A MAN

DON'T YOU NEVER LET A WOMAN GRIEVE YOU
JUST 'CAUSE SHE GOT YOUR WEDDIN' RING
SHE'LL LOVE YOU AND DECEIVE YOU
TAKE YOUR CLOTHES AND LEAVE YOU
'CAUSE A WOMAN IS A SOMETIME THING
— ELLA FITZGERALD

A WOMAN IS A SOMETIME THING

AFTER YOUR LAUGHTER THERE WILL BE TEARS
WHEN YOU'RE IN LOVE, YOU'RE HAPPY
WHEN YOU'RE IN AN ARM, YOU GAZE
THIS DOESN'T LAST ALWAYS
— WENDY RENÉ

AFTER LAUGHTER (COMES TEARS)

AIN'T NO WOMAN LIKE THE ONE I'VE GOT
NO, NO, THEY DON'T COME BETTER
TO MAKE HER HAPPY DOESN'T TAKE A LOT
SHE DON'T ASK FOR THINGS, NO DIAMOND RINGS
— HAMILTON, JOE FRANK & REYNOLDS

AIN'T NO WOMAN (LIKE THE ONE I'VE GOT)

YOU'LL BE GIVEN LOVE
YOU'LL BE TAKEN CARE OF
YOU'LL BE GIVEN LOVE
YOU HAVE TO TRUST IT
— BJÖRK

ALL
IS
FULL
OF
LOVE

WHILE YOU'RE KNOCKING ON ALL THE WRONG DOORS
FOR SOME ANGEL'S TOUCH
YOU THINK SHE'S EVERYTHING YOU'RE DREAMING OF
THE TROUBLE IS THOSE ANGELS NEVER FALL IN LOVE
— THE BANGLES

ANGELS DON'T FALL IN LOVE

YOU MUST REMEMBER THIS
A KISS IS JUST A KISS, A SIGH IS JUST A SIGH
THE FUNDAMENTAL THINGS APPLY
AS TIME GOES BY
– LOUIS ARMSTRONG

AS TIME
GOES BY
(A KISS
IS JUST
A KISS)

SO LET YOUR HEART FLOW
AND SING IT TO YOUR SOUL
BE FREE WITH YOUR LOVE
— SPANDAU BALLET

BE FREE WITH YOUR LOVE

MY POOR HEART WOULD BREAK DEAR IF YOU WERE UNTRUE
ASLEEP OR AWAKE DEAR I DREAM ABOUT YOU
OH YOU ARE MY DARLING YOU'RE ALL THAT I SEE
IF YOU REALLY LOVE ME BE HONEST WITH ME
— BING CROSBY

BE HONEST WITH ME

SHAME ON YOU, YOUR MAMA SAID
SHAME ON YOU, YOU'RE CRYIN' IN BED
SHAME ON YOU, YOU TOLD A LIE
BIG GIRLS DON'T CRY
— THE FOUR SEASONS

BIG

GIRLS

DON'T

CRY

I THINK I'VE FINALLY HAD ENOUGH
I THINK I MAYBE THINK TOO MUCH
I THINK THIS MIGHT BE IT FOR US
BLOW ME ONE LAST KISS
— PINK

BLOW ME (ONE LAST KISS)

I TRY TO LAUGH ABOUT IT
HIDING THE TEARS IN MY EYES
BECAUSE BOYS DON'T CRY
— THE CURE

BOYS DON'T CRY

WELL DON'T YOU KNOW THAT BOYS WILL BE BOYS
BUT BABY I'M A MAN SINCE THE DAY I FOUND YOU
SOMETIMES YOU MAKE ME FEEL
LIKE I GOT A HEART FULL OF TOYS
– THE HOOTERS FEAT. CINDY LAUPER

BOYS
WILL
BE
BOYS

I'M GONNA BREAK INTO YOUR HEART
I'M GONNA CRAWL UNDER YOUR SKIN
I'M GONNA BREAK INTO YOUR HEART
AND FOLLOW TILL I SEE WHERE YOU BEGIN
— IGGY POP

BREAK INTO YOUR HEART

WE'VE SHARED LOVE AND MADE LOVE
IT DOESN'T SEEM TO ME LIKE IT'S ENOUGH
THERE'S JUST NOT ENOUGH OF IT
— BARRY WHITE

CAN'T GET ENOUGH OF YOUR LOVE, BABE

YOU'RE JUST TOO GOOD TO BE TRUE
CAN'T TAKE MY EYES OFF OF YOU
PARDON THE WAY THAT I STARE
THERE'S NOTHING ELSE TO COMPARE
— FRANKIE VALLI

I NEVER MEANT TO HURT YOU
I MUST HAVE BEEN OUT OF MY HEAD
TELL ME YOU STILL WANT ME
CAN'T WE TALK IT OVER IN BED
— OLIVIA NEWTON-JOHN

CAN'T WE TALK IT OVER IN BED

HEAVEN, I'M IN HEAVEN
AND MY HEART BEATS SO THAT I CAN HARDLY SPEAK
AND I SEEM TO FIND THE HAPPINESS I SEEK
WHEN WE'RE OUT TOGETHER DANCING CHEEK TO CHEEK
— ELLA FITZGERALD & LOUIS ARMSTRONG

CHEEK TO CHEEK

JUST DON'T LEAVE ME ALONE HERE
IT'S COLD BABY
COME BACK TO BED
— JOHN MAYER

COME BACK TO BED

GIRL I REFUSE, YOU MUST HAVE ME CONFUSED
WITH SOME OTHER GUY
YOUR BRIDGES WERE BURNED, AND NOW IT'S YOUR TURN
TO CRY, CRY ME A RIVER
— JUSTIN TIMBERLAKE

CRY ME A RIVER

WELL I WISH I REALLY LOVED YOU BUT IT JUST CAN'T BE
AND IF I NEVER SEE YA AGAIN IT'D BE THE SAME TO ME
AND I TRIED TO CRY REAL TEARS FOR YOU
— THE GIZMOS

CRY REAL TEARS

CUDDLE UP A LITTLE CLOSER, LOVEY MINE
CUDDLE UP AND BE MY LITTLE CLINGING VINE
LIKE TO FEEL YOUR CHEEK SO ROSY
LIKE TO MAKE YOU COMFY, COZY
— DORIS DAY

CUDDLE UP A LITTLE CLOSER

FOLLOW MY ADVICE
IF YOU CAN
PUT ALL YOUR DREAMS ON ICE
AND JUST ENJOY THE RIDE
— THE WALKMEN

DANCE WITH YOUR PARTNER

MEN GROW COLD AS GIRLS GROW OLD
WE ALL LOSE OUR CHARM IN THE END
BUT SQUARE CUT OR PEAR SHAPE
THESE ROCKS DON'T LOSE THEIR SHAPE
— CAROL CHANNING

DIAMONDS ARE A GIRL'S BEST FRIEND

IF YOU WANT A DO RIGHT
ALL DAYS WOMAN
YOU'VE GOTTA BE A DO RIGHT
ALL NIGHT MAN
— ARETHA FRANKLIN

DO RIGHT WOMAN, DO RIGHT MAN

PLEASE, LET'S FORGET THE PAST
THE FUTURE LOOKS BRIGHT AHEAD
DON'T BE CRUEL TO A HEART THAT'S TRUE
— ELVIS PRESLEY

DON'T BE CRUEL

IF YOU ARE SHY FOR TOMORROW
YOU'LL BE SHY FOR ONE THOUSAND DAYS
NOW IS YOUR TIME TO SHINE
— THE LIBERTINES

DON'T BE SHY

DON'T BLAME ME
FOR FALLING IN LOVE WITH YOU
I'M UNDER YOUR SPELL
BUT HOW CAN I HELP IT?
— NAT KING COLE

DON'T BLAME ME

DON'T BREAK THE HEART THAT LOVES YOU
HANDLE IT WITH CARE
DON'T BREAK THE HEART THAT NEEDS YOU
DARLING, PLEASE BE FAIR
— CONNIE FRANCIS

DON'T BREAK THE HEART THAT LOVES YOU

PLEASE DON'T EVER BREAK THESE CHAINS OF LOVE
YOU'VE WRAPPED AROUND ME
'CAUSE I'VE BEEN SO HAPPY DARLING
EVER SINCE THE DAY YOU'VE BOUND ME
— DIANA ROSS

(DON'T BREAK THESE) CHAINS OF LOVE

DON'T CHANGE FOR YOU
DON'T CHANGE A THING FOR ME
— INXS

DON'T CHANGE

DON'T CRY NO TEARS AROUND ME
'CAUSE WHEN ALL THE WATER'S GONE
THE FEELING LINGERS ON
OLD TRUE LOVE
AIN'T TOO HARD TO SEE
— NEIL YOUNG

DON'T CRY NO TEARS

DON'T FALL IN LOVE WITH A DREAMER
'CAUSE HE'LL ALWAYS TAKE YOU IN
JUST WHEN YOU THINK YOU'VE REALLY CHANGED HIM
HE'LL LEAVE YOU AGAIN
— KENNY ROGERS FEAT. KIM CARNES

DON'T FALL IN LOVE WITH A DREAMER

SEASONS MUST CHANGE
SEPARATE PATHS, SEPARATE WAYS
IF WE BLAME IT ON ANYTHING
LET'S BLAME IT ON THE RAIN
— MÖTLEY CRÜE

DON'T GO AWAY MAD (JUST GO AWAY)

DON'T GO BREAKING MY HEART
I COULDN'T IF I TRIED
HONEY IF I GET RESTLESS
BABY YOU'RE NOT THAT KIND
— ELTON JOHN & KIKI DEE

DON'T GO BREAKING MY HEART

IT'S YOURS, FOR I DIDN'T HAVE IT
THE MOMENT YOU CAPTURED MY SOUL
FIRST A LITTLE STREAK SHOWED
THEN SLOWLY IT WOVE IT'S WAY RIGHT IN WITH THE GOLD
— GEORGE JONES

DON'T LEAVE WITHOUT TAKING YOUR SILVER

WHEN YOU'RE TIRED OF RACING AND YOU
FOUND YOU NEVER LEFT THE START
COME ON BABY, DON'T LET IT BREAK YOUR HEART
— COLDPLAY

DON'T LET IT BREAK YOUR HEART

I THINK I'M LOSING MY MIND NOW
IT'S IN MY HEAD, DARLING, I HOPE
THAT YOU'LL BE HERE, WHEN I NEED YOU THE MOST
SO DON'T LET ME, DON'T LET ME, DON'T LET ME DOWN
— THE CHAINSMOKERS FEAT. DAYA

DON'T LET ME DOWN

INSTEAD OF DROWNING IN DESPAIR
FOR I FIND SMALL COMFORT IN A BOTTLE
WHEN WE'RE APART
DON'T LET THE TEARDROPS RUST YOUR SHINING HEART
— EVERYTHING BUT THE GIRL

DON'T LET THE TEARDROPS RUST YOUR SHINING HEART

DON'T PUSH LOVE AWAY
YOU KNOW YOU DO
IT'S ALL WE HAVE
IT'S A CHORE HOLDING ONTO A VISION
— THE JULIANA THEORY

DON'T YOU FORGET ABOUT ME
I'LL BE ALONE, DANCING YOU KNOW IT BABY
GOING TO TAKE YOU APART
I'LL PUT US BACK TOGETHER AT HEART, BABY
— SIMPLE MINDS

DON'T YOU (FORGET ABOUT ME)

YOU ALWAYS CARRY THE LOAD WHILE HE'S SITTING AT HOME
DROP YOUR MAN, DROP YOUR MAN
HE'S ALWAYS FUSSING ABOUT ALWAYS CUSSING YOU OUT
DROP YOUR MAN, DROP YOUR MAN
— DANKO JONES

DROP YOUR MAN

EAT YOUR HEART OUT BABY
OH, WON'T YOU GET ME SOMETHING SWEET
EAT YOUR HEART OUT BABY, YEAH
A HOT MESS IS JUST WHAT I NEED
— KISS

WHEN EVEN A FOOL WOULD LET GO
'CAUSE HE KNOWS THAT THERE'S NO USE IN TRYING
EVEN A CHILD WOULD SAY NO
— GAYLE MC CORMICK

EVEN A FOOL WOULD LET GO

DON'T LET YOURSELF GO
EVERYBODY CRIES AND EVERYBODY HURTS SOMETIMES
— R.E.M.

EVERYBODY HURTS

EVERYBODY LOVES A WINNER
BUT WHEN YOU LOSE, YOU LOSE ALONE
— WILLIAM BELL

EVERYBODY LOVES A WINNER

EVERYBODY NEEDS SOMEBODY TO LOVE (SOMEONE TO LOVE)
SWEETHEART TO MISS (SWEETHEART TO MISS)
SUGAR TO KISS (SUGAR TO KISS)
— THE BLUES BROTHERS

EVERYBODY NEEDS SOMEBODY TO LOVE

EVERYBODY'S CHEATING ON THE ONE THEY LOVE
EVERYBODY'S LOOKING FOR THE SUMMER SUN
NO, I BELIEVE I'LL LOVE YOU 'TIL MY LIFE IS DONE
I'LL LIVE YOUR LIES AND ALIBIS
— RICK SPRINGFIELD

EVERYBODY'S CHEATING

FOOLS RUSH IN WHERE WISE MEN NEVER GO
BUT WISE MEN NEVER FALL IN LOVE SO HOW ARE THEY TO KNOW
WHEN WE MET I FELT MY LIFE BEGAN
SO OPEN UP YOUR HEART AND LET THIS FOOL RUSH IN
— BOB CROSBY

FOOLS RUSH IN

FOR EVERY PRINCE THERE'S A PRINCESS
FOR EVERY JOE THERE'S A JOAN
AND IF YOU WAIT, YOU WILL MEET THE MATE
BORN FOR YOU ALONE, HAPPY TO BE YOUR OWN
— SHIRLEY BASSEY

FOR EVERY MAN THERE'S A WOMAN

DON'T FOOL YOURSELF, SHE WAS HEARTACHE FROM THE MOMENT
THAT YOU MET HER
MY HEART IS FROZEN STILL AS I TRY TO FIND THE WILL TO
FORGET HER, SOMEHOW
— JEFF BUCKLEY

FORGET HER

FUCK FOREVER
IF YOU DON'T MIND
— BABYSHAMBLES

FUCK
FOREVER

SUCKING ON MY TITTIES LIKE YOU WANTED ME
CALLING ME, ALL THE TIME LIKE BLONDIE
CHECK OUT MY CHRISSY BEHIND
IT'S FINE ALL OF THE TIME
LIKE SEX ON THE BEACHES
— PEACHES

FUCK
THE
PAIN
AWAY

YOU'RE AN UNTAMED YOUTH
THAT'S THE TRUTH
WITH YOUR CLOAK FULL OF EAGLES
YOU'RE DIRTY SWEET
AND YOU'RE MY GIRL
— T. REX

```
WE'RE UP ALL NIGHT TO THE SUN
WE'RE UP ALL NIGHT TO GET SOME
WE'RE UP ALL NIGHT FOR GOOD FUN
WE'RE UP ALL NIGHT TO GET LUCKY
- DAFT PUNK FEAT. PHARRELL WILLIAMS
```

DON'T PUSH LOVE AWAY

IT'S A SLOW JOB FALLING IN LOVE
IT'S A SLOW JOB
DON'T RUSH GOOD THINGS TONIGHT
— TINA TURNER

DON'T RUSH THE GOOD THINGS

SAVE THAT KISS FOR THE MORNIN' LIGHT
TILL THE SUN COMES UP, WE'LL BE LOST IN US
DON'T SAY GOODBYE
THE NIGHT WAS MADE FOR LOVE, LOVE
— SERGIO MENDES FEAT. JOHN LEGEND

DON'T SAY GOODBYE

DON'T SPEAK
I KNOW JUST WHAT YOU'RE SAYING
SO PLEASE STOP EXPLAINING
DON'T TELL ME 'CAUSE IT HURTS
— NO DOUBT

DON'T SPEAK

BEEN SO LONG SINCE I FOUND SOMEONE
YOU CAME AS SOME SURPRISE
BUT I KNEW YOU WERE MEANT FOR ME
WHEN I LOOKED INTO YOUR EYES
— BOYZONE

DON'T STOP LOOKING FOR LOVE

DON'T TALK JUST KISS
LET YOUR TONGUE FOOL AROUND
LET'S FOOL AROUND
— RIGHT SAID FRED

GET LUCKY

WELL, I'M BEGGING YOU ONE MORE TIME, BABY
DOWN ON BENDED KNEES
PLEASE, PLEASE COME BACK HOME
AND GIVE MY POOR HEART EASE
— RAY CHARLES

GET ON
THE
RIGHT
TRACK
BABY

I WON'T LET THAT LOVE ESCAPE ME ONCE AGAIN
I'M GONNA GET THAT LOVE AND MAKE IT MINE
— THOMPSON TWINS

GET
THAT
LOVE

JUST GIMME SOME KIND OF SIGN GIRL
OH MY BABY
TO SHOW ME THAT YOU'RE MINE GIRL
ALL RIGHT
— BRENTON WOOD

GIMME
LITTLE
SIGN

GIRLS, YOU CAN'T DO WHAT THE GUYS DO, NO
AND STILL BE A LADY
— DUSTY SPRINGFIELD

GIRLS CAN'T DO WHAT THE GUYS DO

AND WHEN I SEE HIM IN THE STREET
MY HEART TAKES A LEAP AND SKIPS A BEAT
GONNA WALK RIGHT UP TO HIM
GIVE HIM A GREAT BIG KISS
— THE SHANGRI-LAS

GIVE THE WOMEN WHAT THEY WANT
DON'T SAY NO
— THE ISLEY BROTHERS

GIVE THE
WOMEN
WHAT
THEY
WANT

GO, GO WHERE YOUR HEART BELIEVES
YOUR MEMORIES ARE WAITING
IT'S THE ONLY WAY TO FIND OUT WHO YOU ARE
— CHRIS DE BURGH

GO WHERE YOUR HEART BELIEVES

IF I HAD MY CHOICE OF WOMEN
I'D PICK THE ONES THAT'D GO ANYWHERE
ALL GOOD GIRLS THEY GO TO HEAVEN
ALL BAD GIRLS GO EVERYWHERE THEY LIKE
— CHEAP TRICK

GOOD GIRLS GO TO HEAVEN (BAD GIRLS GO EVERYWHERE)

I SAY GOODBYE TO ROMANCE
GOODBYE TO FRIENDS, I TELL YOU
GOODBYE TO ALL THE PAST
— OZZY OSBOURNE

GOODBYE TO ROMANCE

LOVE'S JUST LIKE A FINE OLD VINTAGE WINE
BABY, GOTTA GIVE IT TIME
— THE MONKEES

GOTTA GIVE IT TIME

WELL YOU ASK ME IF I'LL FORGET MY BABY
I GUESS I WILL, SOMEDAY
I DON'T LIKE IT BUT I GUESS THINGS HAPPEN THAT WAY
— JOHNNY CASH

GUESS THINGS HAPPEN THAT WAY

I'M FALLIN' HEART OVER HEAD
OVER HEART OVER HEAD OVER YOU
WHERE DID YOU GET YOUR TOUCH?
— BETTE MIDLER

154

HEART OVER HEAD

OH NO, DON'T BE SHY
YOU DON'T HAVE TO GO BLIND
HOLD ME, THRILL ME, KISS ME, KILL ME
— U2

HOLD ME, THRILL ME, KISS ME, KILL ME

IT'S MY HEART THAT SEES, NOT MY EYES
AND IF YOU LISTEN CLOSE I'LL TELL YOU WHY
HOME IS WHERE THE HEART IS
AND MY HEART IS AT HOME WITH YOU
— ELVIS PRESLEY

HOME
IS WHERE
THE HEART
IS

DON'T WANNA CLOSE MY EYES
I DON'T WANNA FALL ASLEEP
'CAUSE I'D MISS YOU, BABY
AND I DON'T WANNA MISS A THING
— AEROSMITH

I DON'T WANT WANT TO MISS A THING

MAMA TOLD ME DON'T TRY
WHEN I SAID I WAS GONNA BE
THE GIRL WHO'D MAKE YOU REALIZE
ONE LOVE WAS ALL YOU NEED
— THE SUPREMES

I GOT
HURT
(TRYING TO
BE THE
ONLY GIRL
IN YOUR LIFE)

THEY SAY WE'RE YOUNG AND WE DON'T KNOW
WE WON'T FIND OUT UNTIL WE'RE GROWN
WELL I DON'T KNOW IF ALL THAT'S TRUE
'CAUSE YOU GOT ME, AND BABY I GOT YOU
— SONNY & CHER

I GOT YOU BABE

WELL I HOPE THAT I DON'T FALL IN LOVE WITH YOU
'CAUSE FALLING IN LOVE JUST MAKES ME BLUE
— TOM WAITS

I HOPE THAT I DON'T FALL IN LOVE WITH YOU

I WANNA DANCE WITH SOMEBODY
I WANNA FEEL THE HEAT WITH SOMEBODY
YEAH! I WANNA DANCE WITH SOMEBODY
WITH SOMEBODY WHO LOVES ME
— WHITNEY HOUSTON

I WANNA DANCE WITH SOMEBODY (WHO LOVES ME)

I WANNA HOLD YOU BABY
I WANNA FEEL YOU RIGHT
I WANNA FEEL YOU BABY
KISS YOU ALL THROUGH THE NIGHT
— HASIL ADKINS

I WANNA
KISS KISS
KISS YOUR
LIPS

I GOTTA SLEEP IN YOUR ARMS
WRAP ME UP IN YOUR HANDS
I'LL FINALLY FEEL CALM
AND FINALLY JUST RELAX
— THE MODERN LOVERS

I
WANNA
SLEEP
IN YOUR
ARMS

OH PLEASE, SAY TO ME
YOU'LL LET ME BE YOUR MAN
AND PLEASE, SAY TO ME
YOU'LL LET ME HOLD YOUR HAND
– THE BEATLES

I WANT TO HOLD YOUR HAND

YOU KNOW IF IT COMES TRUE
I'LL BE SO GOOD TO YOU
I'LL NEVER TREAT YOU CRUEL
AS LONG AS I'VE GOT YOU AROUND
— RAMONES

I WANT YOU AROUND

OH BABY, GIVE ME ONE MORE CHANCE
TO SHOW YOU THAT I LOVE YOU
WON'T YOU PLEASE LET ME BACK IN YOUR HEART
OH DARLIN', I WAS BLIND TO LET YOU GO
— THE JACKSON FIVE

I WANT YOU BACK

I'LL SHINE UP THE OLD BROWN SHOES
PUT ON A BRAND-NEW SHIRT
I'LL GET HOME EARLY FROM WORK
IF YOU SAY THAT YOU LOVE ME
— CHEAP TRICK

TONIGHT, I WANNA LAY IT AT YOUR FEET
'CAUSE GIRL I WAS MADE FOR YOU
AND GIRL YOU WERE MADE FOR ME
— KISS

I WAS MADE FOR LOVING YOU

IF LOVING YOU IS WRONG I DON'T TO BE RIGHT
IF BEING RIGHT MEANS BEING WITHOUT YOU
I'D RATHER LIVE A WRONGDOING LIFE
— BOBBY BLAND

IF
LOVING
YOU IS
WRONG
(I DON'T
WANT TO
BE RIGHT)

A PRETTY WOMAN MAKES HER HUSBAND LOOK SMALL
AND VERY OFTEN CAUSES HIS DOWNFALL
AS SOON AS HE MARRIES HER
THEN SHE STARTS TO DO
THE THINGS THAT WILL BREAK HIS HEART
— JIMMY SOUL

IF YOU
WANT TO
BE HAPPY
(GET AN
UGLY GIRL
TO MARRY
YOU)

WHAT DO YOU GET WHEN YOU KISS A GUY?
YOU GET ENOUGH GERMS TO CATCH PNEUMONIA
AFTER YOU DO, HE'LL NEVER PHONE YA
I'LL NEVER FALL IN LOVE AGAIN
— DIONNE WARWICK

I'LL NEVER FALL IN LOVE AGAIN

THE SILENCE OF A FALLING STAR
LIGHTS UP A PURPLE SKY
AND AS I WONDER WHERE YOU ARE
I'M SO LONESOME I COULD CRY
— HANK WILLIAMS

I'M SO LONESOME I COULD CRY

YOU SAY YOU'RE LOOKIN' FOR SOMEONE
WHO'S NEVER WEAK BUT ALWAYS STRONG
TO PROTECT YOU AN' DEFEND YOU
WHETHER YOU ARE RIGHT OR WRONG
— BOB DYLAN

IT AIN'T ME BABE

WHERE THE SUN ALWAYS SHINES
THERE'S A DESERT BELOW
IT TAKES A LITTLE RAIN
TO MAKE LOVE GROW
— THE OAK RIDGE BOYS

IT TAKES A LITTLE RAIN (TO MAKE LOVE GROW)

OH I CAN REMEMBER HOW HER LOVE CAN BE
AND I CAN'T FORGET THE WAY SHE LOOKS AT ME
IF YOU GOT A GIRL I'M SURE SHE UNDERSTANDS
IT TAKES A WOMAN'S LOVE TO MAKE A MAN
— KANSAS

IT TAKES A WOMAN'S LOVE (TO MAKE A MAN)

THIS IS A MAN'S WORLD, THIS IS A MAN'S WORLD
BUT IT WOULDN'T BE NOTHING
NOTHING WITHOUT A WOMAN OR A GIRL
— JAMES BROWN

IT'S A MAN'S MAN'S MAN'S WORLD

SHE PUT ME OUT, IT WAS A PITY HOW I CRIED
BUT THE TABLES TURNED AND NOW IT'S HER TURN TO CRY
BECAUSE I USED TO LOVE HER BUT IT'S ALL OVER NOW
— ROD STEWART

IT'S ALL OVER NOW

OH, A HOUSE IS JUST A HOUSE WITHOUT A MAN
HE IS THE NECESSARY EVIL IN YOUR PLAN
JUST A KNIGHT IN SHINING ARMOR
WHO IS SOMETHING OF A CHARMER
— DELLA REESE

IT'S SO NICE TO HAVE A MAN AROUND THE HOUSE

IT'S TOO LATE NOW FOR YOU TO SAY YOU'RE SORRY
IT'S TOO LATE NOW FOR YOU TO MAKE AMENDS
YOU'RE GONNA PAY FOR ALL THE LIES YOU TOLD ME
WELL DON'T APOLOGIZE 'CAUSE IT'S TOO LATE
— THE KINKS

IT'S TOO LATE

JEALOUSY WILL GET YOU NOWHERE
YOU OUGHTA KNOW BY NOW
YOU'RE JUST DIGGING A HOLE THAT WON'T LET YOU GO
AND YOU MIGHT NOT WANT TO ANYHOW
— WHITE HASSLE

JEALOUSY (WILL GET YOU)

BABY, YOU DON'T GOTTA LIE TO ME, NO
JUST BE A MAN ABOUT IT
IF YOU WANNA LEAVE GO ON
JUST BE A MAN ABOUT IT
— TONI BRAXTON

JUST BE A MAN ABOUT IT

YOU DON'T HAVE TO TELL ME OF YOUR DESIRE
'CAUSE I'LL NEVER HEAR YOU WHILE MY HEART'S ON FIRE
SO DON'T EXPLAIN KISS ME
JUST KISS ME AND I'LL KNOW
— DEAN MARTIN

JUST
KISS
ME

LISTEN, YOU BETTER KEEP THE WOMAN YOU GOT
I KNOW THE OTHER ONE LOOKS GOOD TO YA
BUT SHE MIGHT NOT BE AS GOOD AS SHE LOOKS
— JOE TEX

KEEP
THE ONE
YOU GOT

YOU DON'T HAVE TO BE COOL
TO RULE MY WORLD
AIN'T NO PARTICULAR SIGN I'M MORE COMPATIBLE WITH
I JUST WANT YOUR EXTRA TIME AND YOUR KISS
— PRINCE

KISS

I'LL GIVE YOU THE GIFT THAT KEEPS ON GIVIN'
IT WON'T COST YOU ANY MONEY
THEN SHE GRABBED ME BY THE EARS AND SAID
KISS ME WHERE IT SMELLS FUNNY
— BLOODHOUND GANG

SO WHAT'S ONE LITTLE KISS
ONE TINY LITTLE TOUCH
AAAH, HE'S WANTING IT SO MUCH
I SWEAR THAT THIS IS ROYAL BLOOD
— PETER GABRIEL

KISS THAT FROG

HOW CAN I LEARN TO SAY GOODBYE
TO THE ONLY LIFE I EVER KNEW?
LEARN TO SAY GOODBYE TO YOU?
— DUSTY SPRINGFIELD

LEARN TO SAY GOODBYE

REVEALED, EACH PART HAS NOW BEEN PLAYED
YOUR BEAUTY WILL NOT FADE
SO CLING TO ME, FULFILL YOUR VOW
LET US NOW MAKE LOVE
— GENESIS

LET
US NOW
MAKE
LOVE

WHEN YOUR WHOLE WORLD IS SINKIN'
COME TO MY WAY OF THINKIN'
LET YOUR HEART RULE YOUR HEAD TONIGHT
— BRIAN MAY

LET YOUR HEART RULE YOUR HEAD

LET YOUR LOVE FLY LIKE A BIRD ON A WING
AND LET YOUR LOVE BIND YOU TO ALL LIVING THINGS
— THE BELLAMY BROTHERS

LET
YOUR
LOVE
FLOW

YOU JUST NEVER KNOW
HOW TOMORROW WILL GO
SO LET'S MAKE SURE WE KISS GOODBYE
— VINCE GILL

LET'S
MAKE
SURE WE
KISS
GOODBYE

```
NO MORE ANYTHING TO DRINK
LEAVE THOSE DISHES IN THE SINK
WHAT'S TO DO ABOUT IT
SIMPLY NIGHTY-NIGHT AND GO TO SLEEP
— DEAN MARTIN
```

LET'S PUT OUT THE LIGHTS (AND GO TO SLEEP)

LET'S SPEND THE NIGHT TOGETHER
DON'T HANG ME UP AND DON'T LET ME DOWN
(DON'T LET ME DOWN)
WE COULD HAVE FUN JUST GROOVIN' AROUND
AROUND AND AROUND
— THE ROLLING STONES

LET'S SPEND THE NIGHT TOGETHER

LET'S TALK ABOUT SEX, BABY
LET'S TALK ABOUT YOU AND ME
LET'S TALK ABOUT ALL THE GOOD THINGS
AND THE BAD THINGS THAT MAY BE
— SALT'N'PEPA

LET'S TALK ABOUT SEX

LIE DOWN HERE & BE MY GIRL
AND LET IT ALL COME DOWN TONIGHT
WE CAN SHINE, SHINE
— NICK CAVE & THE BAD SEEDS

LIE DOWN HERE (& BE MY GIRL)

LISTEN TO YOUR HEART
THERE'S NOTHING ELSE YOU CAN DO
— ROXETTE

LONELY WOMEN MAKE GOOD LOVERS
THEY ALL HAVE MERCY FOR GOOD LOOKIN' SMOOTH TALKIN' MEN
— STEVE WARINER

LONELY WOMEN MAKE GOOD LOVERS

COME TASTE MY LOVE BABY
BLOOD MAKES ME HARD TO RESIST
MY SOUL BURNS LIKE FIRE
KISS MY HUNGRY LIPS VAMPIRE!
— GRACE JONES

LOVE
BITES

THERE'S POOLS ALONG THIS RIVER
WHERE THE SUN WILL NEVER SHINE
AS I LOOK INTO MY HEART AND COUNT MY LOSS I FIND
THAT LOVE IS A LONESOME RIVER
RUNNING THROUGH THE LONESOME MIND
— GLEN CAMPBELL

LOVE IS A LONESOME RIVER

LOVE IS A SHIELD, TO HIDE BEHIND
LOVE IS A FIELD, TO GROW INSIDE
AND WHEN I SOMETIMES CLOSE MY EYES
MY MIND STARTS SPINNING ROUND
— CAMOUFLAGE

LOVE
IS A
SHIELD

```
ALL WE NEED IS LOVE
LOVE IS ALL WE NEED
LOVE UNDERNEATH THE TREE
LOVE IS EVERYTHING
— JOHNNY MATHIS
```

LOVE
IS
EVERYTHING

LOVE IS THAT KIND OF GAME
WHERE THE RULE IS NOT THE KING
SOME PEOPLE GET LUCKY AND WIN
BUT LOSER HAS TO PAY IN THE END
— WILLIE WRIGHT

LOVE IS EXPENSIVE

```
LOVE IS LIKE OXYGEN
YOU GET TOO MUCH, YOU GET TOO HIGH
NOT ENOUGH AND YOU'RE GONNA DIE
LOVE GETS YOU HIGH
— SWEET
```

LOVE IS LIKE OXYGEN

HEY, THE SOONER WE REALIZE
WE COVER OURSELVES WITH LIES
BUT UNDERNEATH WE'RE NOT SO TOUGH
AND LOVE IS NOT ENOUGH
— NINE INCH NAILS

LOVE IS NOT ENOUGH

SURE WOULD LIKE TO PICK UP RIGHT WHERE WE LEFT OFF
I'M GONNA PACK MY BAGS AND CATCH ME AN EARLY FLIGHT
LOVE IS ON MY MIND, SO I'LL BE HOME TONIGHT
— NATALIE COLE

LOVE IS ON THE WAY

HERE COME THE BLUE SKIES, HERE COMES THE SPRINGTIME
WHEN THE RIVERS RUN HIGH AND THE TEARS RUN DRY
WHEN EVERYTHING THAT DIES SHALL RISE
LOVE, LOVE, LOVE IS STRONGER THAN DEATH
— THE THE

LOVE IS
STRONGER
THAN
DEATH

DIM THE LIGHTS, YOU CAN GUESS THE REST
OH OH CATCH THAT BUZZ
LOVE IS THE DRUG I'M THINKING OF
— ROXY MUSIC

WE HEAR THE MYSTERY
LOVE IS THE LANGUAGE OF THE HEART
OH SPEAK LOW WHEN YOU SPEAK TO ME
— JENNIFER RUSH

LOVE IS THE LANGUAGE (OF THE HEART)

LOVE IS WHAT YOU MAKE IT
YOU CAN'T MAKE OR BREAK IT
SO DON'T YOU RUN
— THE GRASS ROOTS

LOVE IS WHAT YOU MAKE IT

LIKE ROMEO AND JULIET
YOU TWO MADE A PACT OF DEATH
LIKE THE NEEDLE THAT YA USED
SID AND NANCY WERE BORN TO LOSE
— RAMONES

LOVE KILLS

LOVE ME TENDER, LOVE ME SWEET
NEVER LET ME GO
YOU HAVE MADE MY LIFE COMPLETE
AND I LOVE YOU SO
— ELVIS PRESLEY

LOVE
ME
TENDER

I'LL TAKE WHAT SCARES YOU AND HOLD IT DEEP INSIDE
AND IF YOU ASK ME WHY
I'M WITH YOU AND WHY I'LL NEVER LEAVE
MY LOVE WILL SHOW YOU EVERYTHING
— JENNIFER LOVE HEWITT

LOVE
WILL SHOW
YOU
EVERYTHING

WHY IS THE BEDROOM SO COLD?
YOU'VE TURNED AWAY ON YOUR SIDE
IS MY TIMING THAT FLAWED?
OUR RESPECT RUNS SO DRY
— JOY DIVISION

LOVE
WILL
TEAR US
APART

WHEN WE WENT TO BED, HE LAY LIKE HE WAS DEAD
MAIDS WHEN YOU'RE YOUNG NEVER WED AN OLD MAN
— THE DUBLINERS

MAIDS WHEN YOU'RE YOUNG NEVER WED AN OLD MAN

ALL YOU GIRLS 'ROUND THE WORLD
LOOKIN' FOR A GUY WHO'S A REAL GO-GETTER
EVERY GUY GRAB A GIRL
LOVE HER LIKE A MAN, MAKE HER FEEL A LOT BETTER
— DEF LEPPARD

MAKE LOVE LIKE A MAN

MAKE JUST ONE HEART THE HEART YOU SING TO
ONE SMILE THAT CHEERS YOU
ONE FACE THAT LIGHTS WHEN IT NEARS YOU
— ARETHA FRANKLIN

MAKE
SOMEONE
HAPPY

MONEY CAN'T BUY LOVE
YOU BETTER GET THAT THROUGH YOUR HEAD
OR ELSE IT'S GONNA BE LOST
ON A CERTAIN SIDE OF YOUR BED
— ROY BROWN

MONEY CAN'T BUY LOVE

LOVE CAN BREAK YOUR HEART BUT NOT TONIGHT
LET THE MUSIC PLAY, LET THE MUSIC PLAY
— STAN WALKER

MUSIC WON'T BREAK YOUR HEART

NEAR, FAR, WHEREVER YOU ARE
I BELIEVE THAT THE HEART DOES GO ON
ONCE MORE YOU OPEN THE DOOR
AND YOU'RE HERE IN MY HEART
AND MY HEART WILL GO ON AND ON
— CÉLINE DION

MY HEART WILL GO ON

I KEEP SEARCHIN' FOR YOU DARLIN'
SEARCHIN' EVERYWHERE I GO
AND WHEN I FIND YOU THERE'S GONNA BE
JUST ONE THING THAT YOU GOTTA KNOW
ONE THING YOU GOTTA KNOW
MY LOVE, LOVE, LOVE, LOVE, LOVE, LOVE
WILL NOT LET YOU DOWN
— BRUCE SPRINGSTEEN

MY LOVE WILL NOT LET YOU DOWN

IT'S THAT SAME OLD DIZZY HANG-UP
I CAN'T DO WITH YOU OR WITHOUT
TELL ME WHY IS IT SO?
I DON'T WANNA LET YOU GO!
— THE JACKSON FIVE

NEVER CAN SAY GOODBYE

NEVER GONNA GIVE YOU UP
NO MATTER HOW YOU TREAT ME
NEVER GONNA GIVE YOU UP
SO DON'T YOU THINK OF LEAVIN'
— THE BLACK KEYS

I'LL NEVER STOP LOVING YOU THIS LIFE
MAYBE I'M WRONG MAYBE I'M RIGHT
— COLD CHISEL

NEVER STOP LOVING YOU

WATCH OUT, HE'S GONNA BREAK YOUR HEART
TRY TO UNDERSTAND
NEVER WEAR MASCARA
WHEN YOU LOVE A MARRIED MAN
— THE HANK WANGFORD BAND

NEVER WEAR MASCARA (WHEN YOU LOVE A MARRIED MAN)

I REMEMBER EVERY SINGLE THING YOU SAID TO ME
YOU PLAYED THE MAN AND I WAS CALVARY
AND YOU SAID, AH YOU SAID
NEW LOVE GROWS ON TREES
— PETE DOHERTY

NEW
LOVE
GROWS
ON
TREES

SO TIRED, TIRED OF THIS DRAMA
NO MORE, NO MORE
I WANNA BE FREE
I'M SO TIRED, SO TIRED
— MARY J. BLIGE

NO MORE MORE DRAMA

ENOUGH IS ENOUGH, IS ENOUGH
I WANT HIM OUT, I WANT HIM OUT THAT DOOR NOW
— DONNA SUMMER & BARBARA STREISAND

NO MORE TEARS (ENOUGH IS ENOUGH)

ONE IS THE LONELIEST NUMBER THAT YOU'LL EVER DO
TWO CAN BE AS BAD AS ONE
IT'S THE LONELIEST NUMBER SINCE THE NUMBER ONE
— HARRY NILSSON

ONE
(IS THE
LONELIEST
NUMBER)

ONE THING LEADS TO ANOTHER
AND BEFORE YOU KNOW, YOU'RE IN TROUBLE
— BETTY WRIGHT

ONE THING LEADS TO ANOTHER

TRY TO BE SURE RIGHT FROM THE START
YES ONLY LOVE CAN BREAK YOUR HEART
— STEPHEN STILLS

ONLY LOVE CAN BREAK YOUR HEART

ONLY ONE MORE KISS
I DIDN'T MEAN TO HURT YOU LITTLE GIRL
LET'S MAKE IT ONE TO REMEMBER
— PAUL MC CARTNEY

ONLY ONE MORE KISS

I HOLD THE LOCK AND YOU HOLD THE KEY
OPEN YOUR HEART TO ME, DARLIN'
I'LL GIVE YOU LOVE IF YOU, YOU TURN THE KEY
— MADONNA

OPEN YOUR HEART

YOU ALONE ARE THE LIVING THING THAT KEEPS ME ALIVE
AND TOMORROW IF I'M HERE WITHOUT YOUR LOVE
YOU KNOW I CAN'T SURVIVE
— ANDY GIBB

(OUR LOVE) DON'T THROW IT AWAY

IT TOOK A WHILE BEFORE I FIGURED IT OUT
THE WAY THE GIRLS TALK, IT'S ALL OVER SCHOOL
I STUCK AROUND THROUGH ALL OF MY DOUBT
BUT THEN YOU WENT AND YOU BROKE THE GOLDEN RULE
OOH, YOU KNOW I PLAY THE FOOL
— RIVAL SONS

PLAY THE FOOL

I DO ALL THE PLEASING WITH YOU, IT'S SO HARD TO REASON
WITH YOU, WHOAH YEAH, WHY DO YOU MAKE ME BLUE
— THE BEATLES

PLEASE PLEASE ME

YOU SEE IT'S GETTING LATE
OH, PLEASE DON'T HESITATE
PUT A LITTLE LOVE IN YOUR HEART
AND THE WORLD WILL BE A BETTER PLACE
— JACKIE DESHANNON

PUT A
LITTLE
LOVE IN
YOUR
HEART

SOMETIMES I WISH I COULD TURN BACK TIME
IMPOSSIBLE AS IT MAY SEEM
BUT I WISH I COULD SO BAD BABY
QUIT PLAYIN' GAMES WITH MY HEART
— BACKSTREET BOYS

QUIT PLAYIN' GAMES (WITH MY HEART)

REACH OUT, COME ON GIRL REACH ON OUT FOR ME
I'LL BE THERE TO LOVE AND COMFORT YOU
AND I'LL BE THERE TO CHERISH AND CARE FOR YOU
— FOUR TOPS

REACH OUT I'LL BE THERE

DO YOU REMEMBER
HOW IT ALL BEGAN
IT JUST SEEMED LIKE HEAVEN
SO WHY DID IT END?
— MICHAEL JACKSON

REMEMBER THE TIME

AND DON'T FORGET WHO'S TAKING YOU HOME
AND IN WHOSE ARMS YOU'RE GONNA BE
OH DARLING, SAVE THE LAST DANCE FOR ME
— HARRY NILSSON

SAVE
THE LAST
DANCE
FOR ME

WHEN YOU CRY IN THE NIGHT
FOR THE LOVE THAT YOU NEED
BABY, SAVE UP YOUR TEARS
CAUSE YOU'LL BE CRYIN' OVER ME
— BONNIE TYLER

SAY IT AIN'T SO
YOUR DRUG IS A HEARTBREAKER
SAY IT AIN'T SO
MY LOVE IS A LIFE TAKER
– WEEZER

IT'S ALL GONNA BE OK
GET USED TO IT DON'T LOSE YOUR HEAD
IT'S ALL GONNA BE THE SAME
SHE KNOWS SEND A MESSAGE TO HER
— BECK

SEND A MESSAGE TO HER

WE BOTH KNOW WE AIN'T KIDS NO MORE
SEND MY LOVE TO YOUR NEW LOVER
TREAT HER BETTER
— ADELE

SEND MY LOVE (TO YOUR NEW LOVER)

I BEEN OUTTA IN THESE STREETS AND I HAD LEARNED THAT
EVERY GIRL I GAVE MY LOVIN' TO WAS ONLY A SUBSTITUTE
— TREY SONGZ

SEX AIN'T BETTER THAN LOVE

YOU KNOW YOU'RE ALREADY MY OBSESSION
STOP USING SEX AS A WEAPON
LOVE IS MORE THAN A ONE-WAY REFLECTION
— PAT BENATAR

SEX IS A WEAPON

SEX IS NOT ENOUGH
YOU JUST DON'T BLEED ENOUGH FOR ME
KISS ME ONE LAST TIME AGAIN
— OOMPH!

SEX IS NOT ENOUGH

I SAY SEX WILL KEEP US TOGETHER
GET US THROUGH ALL KINDS OF WEATHER
I LOVE THE WAY IT KEEPS GETTING BETTER
— DIVINYLS

SEX WILL KEEP US TOGETHER

SHE WILL KNOW YOUR TROUBLES BETTER THAN I CAN
BUT ONE THING'S FOR SURE
SHE'LL NEVER BE YOUR MAN
— CHRIS CORNELL

SHE'LL NEVER BE YOUR MAN

SHE'S LIKE HEROIN TO ME
SHE CANNOT MISS A VEIN
— THE GUN CLUB

SHE'S LIKE HEROIN TO ME

BABY, HERE I AM
SIGNED, SEALED DELIVERED, I'M YOURS
THEN THAT TIME I WENT AND SAID GOODBYE
NOW I'M BACK AND NOT ASHAMED TO CRY
— STEVIE WONDER

SIGNED, SEALED, DELIVERED I'M YOURS

I'LL SEE YOU PAY, BEFORE I GIVE YOU MY HEART
BABY I'LL DO WITHOUT
THERE'LL COME A DAY
WHEN I'LL SMASH YOUR HEART
AND THEN TURN AWAY
— CAT STEVENS

SMASH YOUR HEART

I'M GONNA TELL YOU FOR FREE AND IT WON'T COST A DIME
THERE'S SO MANY WOMEN, SO LITTLE TIME
— ROBERT CRAY

SO MANY
WOMEN,
SO LITTLE
TIME

SOME GUYS HAVE ALL THE LUCK
SOME GUYS HAVE ALL THE PAIN
SOME GUYS GET ALL THE BREAKS
SOME GUYS DO NOTHING BUT COMPLAIN
— ROD STEWART

YOU'RE ON SOMEBODY'S MIND
JUST ALMOST ALL THE TIME
I HOPE YOU MISS ME TOO
SOMEBODY'S MISSING YOU
— DOLLY PARTON

SOMEBODY'S
MISSING
YOU

THOUGH I'VE BEEN HURT BEFORE
IT DOESN'T MEAN I NEVER TRY ANYMORE
TO FIND THAT ONE GIRL I'VE BEEN SEARCHING FOR
AND SHE'LL BE JUST RIGHT FOR ME
— SHALAMAR

SOMEWHERE THERE'S A LOVE

WHEN THE NIGHT HAS COME, AND THE LAND IS DARK
AND THE MOON IS THE ONLY LIGHT WE'LL SEE
NO I WON'T BE AFRAID
JUST AS LONG AS YOU STAND, STAND BY ME
— BEN E. KING

STAND
BY
ME

I'LL GO ANYWHERE WITH YOU
JUST WRAP ME UP IN CHAINS
BUT IF YOU TRY TO GO ALONE
DON'T THINK I'LL UNDERSTAND
— SHAKESPEARS SISTER

STAY

'CAUSE ALL OF THE STARS
ARE FADING AWAY
JUST TRY NOT TO WORRY
YOU'LL SEE THEM SOMEDAY
— OASIS

STOP CRYING YOUR HEART OUT

YOU'RE ALONE ALL THE TIME
DOES IT EVER PUZZLE YOU
HAVE YOU ASKED WHY
YOU SEEM TO FALL IN LOVE AND OUT AGAIN
— THE STYLISTICS

STOP, LOOK, LISTEN (TO YOUR HEART)

IS SHE TALKING DIRTY
GIVE TO ME SWEET SACRED BLISS
YOUR MOUTH WAS MADE TO SUCK MY KISS
— RED HOT CHILI PEPPERS

SUCK MY KISS

```
SO, MY DARLING, PLEASE SURRENDER
ALL YOUR LOVE SO WARM AND TENDER
LET ME HOLD YOU IN MY ARMS, DEAR
WHILE THE MOON SHINES BRIGHT ABOVE
— ELVIS PRESLEY
```

SURRENDER

IF YOU CHANGE YOUR MIND, I'M THE FIRST IN LINE
HONEY I'M STILL FREE
TAKE A CHANCE ON ME
IF YOU NEED ME, LET ME KNOW, GONNA BE AROUND
— ABBA

TAKE A CHANCE ON ME

TAKE CARE OF YOUR WOMAN
DON'T TREAT HER MEAN
MAKE HER FEEL LIKE A WOMAN
AND SHE WON'T EVER LEAVE
— ROY ORBISON

YOU'LL NEVER KNOW I FEEL THE BLOW
I SHOULD GET DOWN ON MY KNEES
BUT I WAS RAISED TO TAKE A STAND
HIDE MY TEARS AND TAKE IT LIKE A MAN
— CONWAY TWITTY

TAKE IT LIKE A MAN

LOVE CAN BE FOREVER
TAKE THE BITTER WITH THE SWEET
WE CAN'T LET RUMORS AFFECT US
WE JUST HAVE TO TRUST
— MUDDY WATERS

TAKE THE BITTER WITH THE SWEET

STEALING KISSES IN THE DARK IS JUST IMMENSE
WHERE CAN YOU GET HALF AS MUCH FOR SIXTY CENTS?
SO TAKE YOUR GIRLIE TO THE MOVIES
IF YOU CAN'T MAKE LOVE AT HOME
— DEAN MARTIN

TAKE YOUR GIRLIE TO THE MOVIES (IF YOU CAN'T MAKE LOVE AT HOME)

BUT IT TAKES TWO TO TANGO
TWO TO REALLY GET THE FEELING OF ROMANCE
LET'S DO THE TANGO, DO THE TANGO
DO THE DANCE OF LOVE
— PEARL BAILEY

TAKES TWO TO TANGO

THESE ARMS ARE WANTING YOU
'CAUSE THESE ARMS AIN'T HOLDING YOU
THESE EYES PUT UP A FIGHT
BUT ONCE AGAIN THESE TEARS ALWAYS WIN
— ALICIA KEYS

TEARS ALWAYS WIN

TEARS DON'T CARE WHO CRIES THEM
THEY DON'T CARE AT ALL
ANYTIME A HEART STARTS BREAKING
THEY WILL FALL AND FALL
— K.D. LANG

TEARS DON'T CARE WHO CRIES THEM

HE WALKS AWAY, THE SUN GOES DOWN
HE TAKES THE DAY BUT I'M GROWN
AND IN YOUR WAY, IN THIS BLUE SHADE
MY TEARS DRY ON THEIR OWN
— AMY WINEHOUSE

TEARS DRY ON THEIR OWN

TELL IT TO YOUR HEART, PLEASE DON'T BE AFRAID
I'M THE ONE WHO LOVES YOU IN EACH AND EVERY WAY
— LOU REED

TELL IT
TO YOUR
HEART

LONESOME GAMBLER
THAT WOMAN WILL LEAD TO HEARTBREAKS
TAKE THE WORD OF ONE
WHO PLAYED AND LOST IN LOVE
— THIN LIZZY

THAT WOMAN'S GONNA BREAK YOUR HEART

YES, WHAT THEY SAY IS TRUE
NO ONE ELSE COULD HURT ME
HURT ME THE WAY YOU DO
— JIMMY RADCLIFFE

THE GREATER THE LOVE, THE DEEPER THE HURT

YOU CAN FIND SOMEONE
AND LIVE YOUR LIFE
PUT AN OLD MEMORY OUT OF YOUR MIND
BUT THE HEART NEVER FORGETS
— LEANN RIMES

THE HEART NEVER FORGETS

GET IT RIGHT
OR JUST LEAVE LOVE ALONE
BECAUSE THE LOVE YOU SAVE TODAY
MAYBE WILL BE YOUR OWN
— JOE TEX

THE LOVE
YOU SAVE
(MAY BE
YOUR
OWN)

YOU KNOW THE NIGHTTIME, OH, IS THE RIGHT TIME
TO BE WITH THE ONE YOU LOVE
— ROOSEVELT SYKES

THE NIGHT TIME IS THE RIGHT TIME

```
THE ONLY THING I WANT
THE ONLY THING I NEED
THE ONLY THING I CHOOSE
THE ONLY THING THAT LOOKS GOOD ON ME IS YOU
— BRYAN ADAMS
```

THE
ONLY THING
THAT
LOOKS GOOD
ON ME
IS YOU

WELL MY SKIES ARE SO CLOUDY GREY
OH, LORD, BABY SINCE YOU, SINCE YOU BEEN AWAY
AH, BUT I KNOW LORD
THAT THE SUN, SUN GONNA SHINE AGAIN
— RAY CHARLES

THE SUN'S GONNA SHINE AGAIN

THE THRILL IS GONE AWAY
YOU KNOW YOU DONE ME WRONG BABY
AND YOU'LL BE SORRY SOMEDAY
— B.B. KING

THERE AIN'T NO HORSE THAT CAN'T BE RODE
THERE AIN'T MANY THINGS THAT CAN'T BE BOUGHT
THERE JUST AIN'T NO MAN THAT CAN'T BE CAUGHT
— JIMMY LEWIS

THERE AIN'T NO MAN THAT CAN'T BE CAUGHT

IT DOESN'T MEAN A THING TO ME
AND IT'S ABOUT TIME YOU SEE
THINGS AIN'T LIKE THEY USED TO BE
— THE BLACK KEYS

THINGS AIN'T LIKE THEY USED TO BE

AND I KNOW YOU'RE NOT THE KIND
WHO LIKES TO CHANGE YOUR MIND
IF YOU'RE UNDECIDED
THINK IT OVER AND BE SURE
— LIZ VERDI

THINK IT OVER

A MAN AND A WOMAN HAD A LITTLE BABY
YES THEY DID
THEY HAD THREE IN THE FAMILY
AND THAT'S A MAGIC NUMBER
— BOB DOROUGH

THREE IS A MAGIC NUMBER

LIKE WAVES IN THE OCEANS, LEAVES IN THE TREES
NOTHING EVER CHANGES BETWEEN YOU AND ME
LOVE IS THE ANSWER
NOW IS THE TIME FOR LOVE
— RANDY CRAWFORD

TIME FOR LOVE

.

HURTS TO BREAK UP
SHE WAS STRONGER
ALL MY FRIENDS SAY
PLEASE DON'T LOVE HER
— BLINK-182

TIME TO BREAK UP

I'LL TRY AGAIN TOMORROW
TRIED IT YESTERDAY
I'M GOING TO LEAVE YOU SOMEDAY
BUT TODAY IS NOT THE DAY
— DEAN MARTIN

TODAY IS NOT THE DAY

TOO MUCH LOVE WILL KILL YOU
IF YOU CAN'T MAKE UP YOUR MIND
TORN BETWEEN THE LOVER
AND THE LOVE YOU LEAVE BEHIND
— QUEEN

DON'T BE SAD, I KNOW YOU WILL
BUT DON'T GIVE UP UNTIL
TRUE LOVE WILL FIND YOU IN THE END
— WILCO

TRUE LOVE WILL FIND YOU IN THE END

SHE MAY BE WEARY, WOMEN DO GET WEARY
WEARING THE SAME SHABBY DRESS
AND WHEN SHE'S WEARY, TRY A LITTLE TENDERNESS
— FRANK SINATRA

TRY
A LITTLE
TENDERNESS

DON'T START NONE OF THAT GRIEVING
'CAUSE THIS TIME SHE'S LEAVING
SHE'S PACKIN' UP HER SUITCASE
TRY TO FIND ANOTHER WOMAN
— THE RIGHTEOUS BROTHERS

TURN IT INTO LOVE
AND OPEN UP YOUR HEART AND YOU'LL
NEVER FEEL ASHAMED IF YOU
TURN IT, TURN IT, TURN IT INTO LOVE
— KYLIE MINOGUE

TURN IT INTO LOVE

SHOULD I REVEAL WHAT I'M FEELING
SHOULD I LOOK INTO YOUR EYES
OR SHOULD I JUST GRAB YOU AND PULL YOU TO ME
SHOULD I SHOULD I SHOULD I
— LISA STANSFIELD

TURN
ME
ON

LOVER, LOVER, WHY IS THERE LIGHT
DID YOU FORGET TO TURN OFF THAT LIGHT
WELL THAT'S ALL RIGHT BUT IT'S WAY TOO BRIGHT
WAY TOO BRIGHT
— LOU REED

TURN OUT THE LIGHT

ONE IS A LONELY NUMBER
IT'S A NUMBER YOU CAN'T DIVIDE
YEAH, BUT LISTEN HONEY
THE NUMBER ONE CAN BE GREAT WHEN IT'S MULTIPLIED
TWO CAN MAKE IT TOGETHER
— TONY AND TANDY

TWO CAN MAKE IT TOGETHER

UN-BREAK MY HEART
SAY YOU'LL LOVE ME AGAIN
UNDO THIS HURT YOU CAUSED
WHEN YOU WALKED OUT THE DOOR
AND WALKED OUT OF MY LIFE
— TONI BRAXTON

UN-BREAK MY HEART

UNCHAIN MY HEART
BABY LET ME GO
UNCHAIN MY HEART
'CAUSE YOU DON'T LOVE ME NO MORE
— RAY CHARLES

UNCHAIN MY HEART

WELL VARIETY IS THE SPICE OF LIFE
THAT'S WHAT THE JUDGE IS GONNA TELL MY WIFE
SHE SAID WHY DID YOU HAVE TO DO IT? WHY YOU SUCH A FOOL?
I CAN'T RESIST TO TRY SOMETHING NEW
— THE DOORS

VARIETY IS THE SPICE OF LIFE

```
I THINK WE BETTER WAIT 'TIL TOMORROW
GIRL WHAT YOU TALKIN' ABOUT?
— THE JIMI HENDRIX EXPERIENCE
```

WAIT UNTIL TOMORROW

WE BELONG TOGETHER, WE BELONG TOGETHER, OH, IT'S TRUE
IT'S GONNA STAY THIS WAY FOREVER, ME AND YOU
— RANDY NEWMAN

WE
BELONG
TOGETHER

ONLY TIME WILL TELL IF I AM RIGHT OR I AM WRONG
WHILE YOU SEE IT YOUR WAY
THERE'S A CHANCE THAT WE MAY FALL APART BEFORE TOO LONG
WE CAN WORK IT OUT
— THE BEATLES

WE HAVE ALL THE TIME IN THE WORLD
JUST FOR LOVE
NOTHING MORE, NOTHING LESS
ONLY LOVE
— LOUIS ARMSTRONG

WE HAVE
ALL THE
TIME
IN THE
WORLD

WE MEET AND WE PART
HEY BABY, IT'S BREAKIN' MY HEART
— THE HOLMES BROTHERS

WE MEET,
WE PART,
WE
REMEMBER

WE'RE NOT SUPPOSED TO BE LOVERS
OR FRIENDS, LIKE THEY'D HAVE US BELIEVE
WE'RE NOT SUPPOSED TO KNOW EACH OTHER
ACCEPT MY APOLOGY
— ADAM GREEN

WE'RE
NOT
SUPPOSED
TO BE
LOVERS

WHEN A MAN LOVES A WOMAN
CAN'T KEEP HIS MIND ON NOTHIN' ELSE
HE'D CHANGE THE WORLD FOR THE GOOD THING HE'S FOUND
— PERCY SLEDGE

WHEN A MAN LOVES A WOMAN

WHY DON'T WE LIVE TOGETHER?
YOU WON'T BELIEVE IN LOVE UNTIL THE DAY YOU TRY
— PET SHOP BOYS

WHY DON'T WE LIVE TOGETHER?

AND NOW I MISS YOU IN SO MANY WAYS
YOU KNOW I MISS YOU FOR SO MANY
LONELY DAYS
OH! WHY DON'T WE TRY AGAIN
— BRIAN MAY

WHY DON'T WE TRY AGAIN

TELL ME WHY DON'T YOU BRING ME FLOWERS?
TELL ME WHY DON'T YOU NOTICE ME?
ANOTHER STRANGER ON A TRAIN, A TIP ROCK IN THE RAIN
IN THE RAIN, IN THE COLD, COLD RAIN
— ROXETTE

WELL, WHY DON'T YOU LOVE ME LIKE YOU USED TO DO?
HOW COME YOU TREAT ME LIKE A WORN OUT SHOE?
MY HAIR'S STILL CURLY, MY EYES ARE STILL BLUE
SO WHY DON'T YOU LOVE ME LIKE YOU USED TO DO?
— HANK WILLIAMS

WHY
DON'T YOU
LOVE ME
(LIKE YOU
USED TO
DO ?)

WILD WOMEN WILL BE THE FIRST ONES
LORD TO LEARN HOW TO FLY
WILD WOMEN NEVER WORRY
WILD WOMEN DON'T GET THE BLUES
— IDA COX

WILD WOMEN DON'T GET THE BLUES

DON'T TAKE FOR GRANTED THE SMILE ON HER FACE
CHECK A LITTLE BIT CLOSER, YOU MIGHT FIND A TEAR TRACE
MAYBE THE GIRL MIGHT NEVER SAY A MUMBLING WORD
BUT YOU GOTTA MAKE SURE THAT HER VOICE IS HEARD
— BOBBY WOMACK

WOMAN'S GOTTA HAVE IT

WORDS, DON'T COME EASY TO ME
HOW CAN I FIND A WAY TO MAKE YOU SEE I LOVE YOU
— F.R. DAVID

WORDS DON'T COME EASY

TO BE IN LOVE, I KNOW IT'S NOT YOUR AMBITION
BUT BEFORE YOU GO, THINK ABOUT MY PROPOSITION
— MARVIN GAYE

YOU AIN'T LIVIN' TILL YOU'RE LOVIN'

YOU ARE THE UNIVERSE
AND THERE AIN'T NOTHIN' YOU CAN'T DO
IF YOU CONCEIVE IT, YOU CAN ACHIEVE IT
THAT'S WHY, I BELIEVE IN YOU, YES I DO
— BRAND NEW HEAVIES

YOU ARE THE UNIVERSE

EVEN MY HANDS BELONG TO YOU
I USE MY HANDS OH TO WORK FOR YOU
EVEN MY HANDS BELONG TO YOU
BECAUSE YOU, YOU BELONG TO ME
— SAM COOKE

YOU BELONG TO ME

YES, I SHINE LIKE THE MORNING SUN
BUT I LOSE ALL MY LUSTER, WHEN WITH A BRONCO BUSTER
OH YOU CAN'T GET A MAN WITH A GUN
— DORIS DAY

YOU CAN'T GET A MAN WITH A GUN

MY MAMA SAID
YOU CAN'T HURRY LOVE
NO, YOU'LL JUST HAVE TO WAIT
SHE SAID LOVE DON'T COME EASY
BUT IT'S A GAME OF GIVE AND TAKE
— PHIL COLLINS

YOU CAN'T HURRY LOVE

OH CAN'T YOU SEE, OH, WELL, YOU MISJUDGED ME
I LOOK LIKE A FARMER BUT I'M A LOVER
YOU CAN'T JUDGE A BOOK BY LOOKING AT THE COVER
— WILLIE DIXON

YOU CAN'T JUDGE A BOOK BY ITS COVER

HE NEVER TOOK YOU TO A CARNIVAL
YOU NEVER HAD A PICNIC IN THE PARK
HE NEVER TOOK YOU DANCIN' AFTER DARK
SEE YOU DESERVE BETTER BABE
— THE ISLEY BROTHERS

YOU
DESERVE
BETTER

YOU DON'T HAVE TO SAY YOU LOVE ME
JUST BE CLOSE AT HAND
YOU DON'T HAVE TO STAY FOREVER
I WILL UNDERSTAND
— DUSTY SPRINGFIELD

YOU DON'T HAVE TO SAY YOU LOVE ME

SHOT THROUGH THE HEART, AND YOU'RE TO BLAME
YOU GIVE LOVE A BAD NAME
I PLAY MY PART AND YOU PLAY YOUR GAME
— BON JOVI

YOU
GIVE
LOVE
A BAD
NAME

GIVE ME GIVE ME GIVE ME WHAT I CRY FOR
YOU KNOW YOU GOT THE BRAND OF KISSES THAT I'D DIE FOR
YOU KNOW YOU MADE ME LOVE YOU
— DEAN MARTIN

YOU MADE ME LOVE YOU (I DIDN'T WANT TO DO IT)

AND NOW THE YOUNG MONSIEUR
AND MADAME HAVE RUNG THE CHAPEL BELL
"C'EST LA VIE", SAY THE OLD FOLKS
IT GOES TO SHOW YOU NEVER CAN TELL
— CHUCK BERRY

YOU NEVER CAN TELL

YOU NEVER MOVE LIKE YOU USED TO DO
POUR IT OUT WHEN YOU'RE FEELIN' BLUE
SOMEBODY MUST HAVE PUT SOME PAIN ON YOU
YOU NEVER CRY LIKE A LOVER
— THE EAGLES

YOU NEVER
CRY
LIKE A
LOVER

AND I'M HERE TO REMIND YOU
OF THE MESS YOU LEFT WHEN YOU WENT AWAY
IT'S NOT FAIR TO DENY ME
OF THE CROSS I BEAR THAT YOU GAVE TO ME
YOU, YOU, YOU OUGHTA KNOW
— ALANIS MORISSETTE

YOU OUGHTA KNOW

GIRL, YOU REALLY GOT ME GOIN'
YOU GOT ME SO I DON'T KNOW WHAT I'M DOIN'
YEAH, YOU REALLY GOT ME NOW
YOU GOT ME SO I CAN'T SLEEP AT NIGHT
— THE KINKS

YOU REALLY GOT ME

```
OH, YOUNG HEARTS RUN FREE
NEVER BE HUNG UP
HUNG UP LIKE MY MAN AND ME
— CANDI STATON
```

YOUNG
HEARTS
RUN
FREE

YOU COULD MAKE ME CRY IF YOU DON'T KNOW
CAN'T REMEMBER WHAT I WAS THINKING OF
YOU MIGHT BE SPOILING ME TOO MUCH LOVE
YER GONNA MAKE ME LONESOME WHEN YOU GO
— BOB DYLAN

YOU'RE GONNA MAKE ME LONESOME WHEN YOU GO

YOU'RE THE ONE AND I WANT YOU TO KNOW
YOU'RE THE ONE THAT THRILLS ME SO
YOU'RE THE ONE, I CAN'T LET YOU GO
YOU'RE THE ONE THAT'S MEANT FOR ME
— BUDDY HOLLY

YOU'RE THE ONE

HOW COULD SHE SAY TO ME
LOVE WILL FIND A WAY
GATHER ROUND ALL YOU CLOWNS
LET ME HEAR YOU SAY
HEY, YOU'VE GOT TO HIDE YOUR LOVE AWAY
— THE BEATLES

YOU'VE GOT TO HIDE YOUR LOVE AWAY

MARCUS KRAFT IS A GRAPHIC
DESIGNER AND ART DIRECTOR
BASED IN ZURICH, SWITZERLAND.
FROM HIS STUDIO, HE REAL-
IZES COMMISSIONED PROJECTS
FOR RENOWNED CLIENTS AS
WELL AS SELF-INITIATED
PROJECTS. HIS FOCUS IS ON
ELABORATE DESIGN CONCEPTS,
EDITORIAL PROJECTS AND
TYPOGRAPHICAL QUALITY. HE
HAS BEEN AWARDED SEVERAL
INTERNATIONAL PRIZES FOR HIS
WORK. IN HIS SPARE TIME,
HE PLAYS THE DRUMS IN A ROCK
BAND.

WWW.MARCUSKRAFT.NET

IMPRINT

CONCEPT, EDITING &
DESIGN BY
MARCUS KRAFT
WWW.MARCUSKRAFT.NET

BIS PUBLISHERS
BUILDING HET SIERAAD
POSTJESWEG 1
1057 DT AMSTERDAM
THE NETHERLANDS
T (31) 020 515 02 30
BIS@BISPUBLISHERS.COM
WWW.BISPUBLISHERS.COM

SPECIAL THANKS TO
DANIEL KUNZ, CHARLOTTE
JÄGGI, BIONDA DIAS & RUDOLF
VAN WEZEL

FIRST PRINTING, 2017

ISBN 978-90-6369-452-4

CHECK OUT THE ACCOMPANYING
BLOG WWW.POPMUSICWISDOM.COM

IF YOU LIKE THIS BOOK,
YOU'LL PROBABLY ALSO
LIKE THE BOOK ‹DON'T EAT
THE YELLOW SNOW› AND THE
POSTCARD BLOCK ‹GET OFF
THE INTERNET›. CHECK IT OUT
AT WWW.BISPUBLISHERS.COM